SMELLY STINKERS

BY VIRGINIA LOH-HAGAN

45TH PARALLEL PRESS

Published in the United States of America by Cherry Lake Publishing Group
Ann Arbor, Michigan
www.cherrylakepublishing.com

Reading Adviser: Beth Walker Gambro, MS Ed., Reading Consultant, Yorkville, IL
Book Designer: Melinda Millward

Photo Credits: Cover: © Ezume Images/Shutterstock; Page 1: © Ezume Images/Shutterstock; Page 5: © Michael Potter11/Shutterstock; Page 6: © Jemini Joseph/Shutterstock, © Jeremy Richards/Shutterstock; Page 7: © Comstock Images/Thinkstock; Page 8: © James Coleman/Shutterstock; Page 10: © Jennifer Mellon Photos/Shutterstock, © Anna Om/Shutterstock; Page 11: © Carolyn/Adobe Stock; Page 12: © Michael Potter11/Shutterstock, © apple2499/Shutterstock; Page 13: © Stefanie Van Der Vinden/Dreamstime; Page 14: © jumbenylon/Adobe Stock; Page 16: © Nicram Sabod/Shutterstock, © bluejava1/Shutterstock; Page 17: © Marcin/Adobe Stock; Page 18: © Frank Fichtmueller/Shutterstock; Page 20: © Henk Bogaard/Shutterstock, © Jaco Wiid/Shutterstock; Page 21: © AndreAnita/Shutterstock; Page 22: © Ezume Images/Shutterstock, © Ryan M. Bolton/Shutterstock; Page 23: © Joy Stein/Shutterstock

Graphic Element Credits: Cover, multiple interior pages: © paprika/Shutterstock, © Silhouette Lover/Shutterstock, © Daria Rosen/Shutterstock, © Wi_Stock/Shutterstock

Library of Congress Cataloging-in-Publication Data

Names: Loh-Hagan, Virginia, author.
Title: Smelly stinkers / written by Virginia Loh-Hagan.
Description: Ann Arbor, Michigan : Cherry Lake Publishing, [2023] | Series: Wild Wicked Wonderful Express. | Audience: Grades 2-3 | Summary: "Eww, what's that smell? Who are the smelly stinkers of the animal kingdom? This book explores the wild, wicked, and wonderful world of the smelliest animals. Series is developed to aid struggling and reluctant young readers with engaging high-interest content, considerate text, and clear visuals. Includes table of contents, glossary with simplified pronunciations, index, sidebars, and author biographies"—Provided by publisher.
Identifiers: LCCN 2022042691 | ISBN 9781668919736 (hardcover) | ISBN 9781668920756 (paperback) | ISBN 9781668922088 (ebook) | ISBN 9781668923412 (pdf)
Subjects: LCSH: Odors—Juvenile literature. | Animal behavior—Juvenile literature.
Classification: LCC QL751.5 .L638 2023 | DDC 591.5—dc23/eng/20220914
LC record available at httA://lccn.loc.gov/2022042691

Cherry Lake Publishing Group would like to acknowledge the work of the Partnership for 21st Century Learning, a Network of Battelle for Kids. Please visit http://www.battelleforkids.org/networks/p21 for more information.

Printed in the United States of America

About the Author
Dr. Virginia Loh-Hagan is an author, university professor, former classroom teacher, and curriculum designer. She conserves water by not showering every day. She doesn't mind being stinky for a good cause. She lives in San Diego with her very tall husband and very naughty dogs.

Table of Contents

Introduction

Animals stink. They have **odors**. Odors are smells. Some animals make odors. They do this on purpose. They often spray to release the odors.

Animals spray for different reasons. They hunt. They protect themselves. They guard their area. They find things.

Some odors are **foul**. Foul means it doesn't smell good. Odors can hurt **victims**' senses. A victim is a person or animal that is harmed. These odors can blind. They can make victims sick. They can confuse victims.

Some animals are extreme stinkers. They're the most exciting stinkers in the animal world!

Animals use odors to benefit them.

Skunks

Skunks are small. They don't need to be big. They don't need to fight. They produce one of the worst smells in the world. You can smell them 1.5 miles (2.4 kilometers) away. They use their scent to scare off **predators**. Predators are animals that hunt other animals.

Predators will only eat skunks if other animals aren't around.

Skunks eat honeybees and wasps. They attack beehives.

Skunks have 2 **anal** scent **glands**. Anal means related to the butt. Glands produce substances used by the body. The glands are the size of walnuts. They're under their large tails. Their spray is powerful. Skunks can spray up to 12 feet (3.7 meters). It causes eyes to tear up. Victims stink for days.

When Animals Attack!

Wolverines have glands that ooze oil. This oil smells musky. It comes out like a cloud. Wolverines are also known as "skunk bears" or "nasty cats." They spray to guard their space. They spray food. They bury their food to eat later. The smell helps them find the food again. It also keeps other animals away.

Hippopotamuses

Hippos live in Africa. Hippos mark their territory in a special way. They spray **dung**. Dung is poop. This action is called "dung showering."

Hippos throw dung at victims. Their dung is created by their **diet**. Diet is what they eat. They eat up to 100 pounds (45 kilograms) of plants. They eat this much every night. The food goes through their stomachs. It breaks down. It becomes a stinky green mess of dung.

Hippos leave 9 tons of dung in the Mara River in Kenya each day.

Hyenas

Hyenas live in Africa. They live in **packs**. Packs are groups. They mark their territory.

Hyenas mark for different reasons. They keep other hyenas away. They guard their space.

Anal glands allow them to mark. These glands make a stinky paste. It's called "hyena butter." It's powerful. It smells for up to 30 days.

Hyenas communicate with smells.

Hyenas can crush bones with their teeth.

They also mark by pooping. Their poop is white. The white color comes from eating a lot of bones!

Humans
Do What?!?

Human skin has more than 2 million sweat glands. These glands release water called sweat. Sweat cools human bodies. It also produces odor when it combines with **bacteria** on the skin. Bacteria are tiny living things that live inside and outside people and animals. Armpits have many sweat glands. They get smelly. That's why humans use deodorants. Some people smell armpits for a living. They are odor testers. They create and improve products that hide body odors.

Musk Oxen

Musk oxen smell of **musk**. Musk smells very strong. It is the smell of some animals. It usually comes from a gland.

This animal's name is tricky. First, musk oxen aren't oxen. They're shaggy. Oxen aren't shaggy. Musk oxen are more like sheep. Second, musk oxen don't have musk glands. Their musk is in their pee.

Musk oxen live in the Arctic. They're powerful land animals.

Musk oxen have thick hairy coats that can keep them warm in the Arctic.

Males shower themselves with pee. They make a big stink. They smell musky. Their smell is very strong. It will make your eyes water.

Musk oxen use their smell. It helps them attract mates.

Did You Know...?

- Chemicals produced by some millipedes can burn or blister human skin. Don't touch millipedes!

- Some people keep skunks as pets. They remove the scent glands. There could be up to 5 million pet skunks in the United States.

Bull Elephants

Bull elephants are male elephants. They stink for one month each year. They go through **musth**. This means they're ready to mate. The males make low rumbles. They make a thick substance. It comes from a small gland on their heads. It's between the eyes and ears. It smells really bad.

But female elephants love the stink. They're attracted to the odors. Stinky means healthy.

Other males don't like the smell. They fight each other.

Bull elephants smell like 1,000 goats in a pen.

Millipedes

Millipedes live in forests. Most people think millipedes are harmless. But they're dangerous when they're in trouble. They create a big stink.

Millipedes make a deadly gas. The gas tastes bad.

Millipedes store the gas. The gas from one millipede can kill a mouse. The gas from 300 millipedes can kill a human.

Millipedes have stink glands called ozopores.

Consider This!

Take a Position! Some humans keep skunks as pets. They remove their scent organs. Do you think this should be allowed? Why or why not?

Think About It! What are some ways that humans change the way they smell? Why do you think humans do this?

Learn More
- **Article:** Animals Around the Globe - "Top 10 Smelliest Animals" by Zee. May 6, 2022: https://www.animalsaroundtheglobe.com/top-10-smelliest-animals/.
- **Book:** Jenkins, Steve. 2018. Stinkiest!: 20 Smelly Animals (Extreme Animals). Clarion Books.

Glossary

anal (AY-nuhl) related to the butt

bacteria (bak-TIHR-ee-uh) tiny living things that live inside and outside people and animals

diet (DYE-uht) what living things eat

dung (DUHNG) poop

foul (FOWL) gross and smelly

glands (GLANDZ) organs that produce substances used by the body

musk (MUHSK) strong-smelling substance produced by animals

musth (MUHST) mating time when bull elephants release a smelly substance

odors (OH-duhrz) smells

packs (PAKS) groups

predators (PREH-duh-turz) animals that hunt other animals for food

victims (VIK-tuhmz) targets of attacks or harm

Index